Personal Journal
Let's Faith it!

Lorraine Jones-Whitfield
Raine Speak Life
Hannah's Heart Ministries

www.lorrainejoneswhitfield.com

HELLO,

Have you ever wanted to do something and didn't know how? How about writing a prayer journal and didn't know exactly where to begin? I had to begin with much prayer and God's leadership. He said to acknowledge Him in all thy ways and He would direct my path (Proverbs 3:6). This may be something very small, but I am hoping that it is a powerful tool to begin your journey with. I thought that it had to be to perfection but, as I began to trust God, the door was open, and he guided my every thought.

I pray that you will enjoy this journal and it will help you to meditate and pray on Him day and night so that your life will be successful in Him.

Raine 2017

www.lorrainejoneswhitfield.com
Hannnahheart7@gmail.com
Women's Book Ministry (Facebook)

NOW FAITH

Now faith is the substance of things hoped for and the evidence of things not seen. (Hebrews 11:1)

Do we have the faith to believe the impossible? Do we have that "now faith" to believe in our healing? Do we have that faith to know God is able? No matter what our situation looks like or feels like, just know God is in it. In the book of Job, we see God allowed but told him not to harm him in any way. God has that hedge of protection around us, but we can't see it in the natural. God is the beginning and the ending of our Faith. **Mark 11:22-24:** "Have faith in God," Jesus answered. "Truly I tell you, if anyone says to this mountain, 'Go, throw yourself into the sea,' and does not doubt in their heart but believes that what they say will happen, it will be done for them.

Therefore, I tell you, whatever you ask for in prayer, believe that you have received it, and it will be yours."

Do we believe the impossible?

"Now faith" is the assurance to know that whatever God says we can do or whatever we need in life it is done. It is because we asked Him and believed that mountain to be moved. There was a time I had a goiter in my throat and the doctors said it was cancerous without testing it. Well, it got bigger to the point that I couldn't swallow and every time I ate or drank I would get choked. The doctors told my husband the next step would be to surgically remove the goiter and we did. That meant that my thyroid would have to be removed and I would take thyroid medication for the rest of my life. To me that would be a blessing because that meant no cancer. Well surgery took place and they removed the thyroid and the goiter. Hallelujah the biopsy came back and no cancer. God is good. Did I believe for the impossible? Well yes. I trusted God in my most trying time. He came through once again.

Do I believe God for my healing?

Yes, I do because He has healed me in the situation with the goiter, through a car accident, and with fibroid tumors and more. I totally trust Him in all things. **Isaiah 53:5:** But he was pierced for our transgressions, he was crushed for our iniquities; the punishment that brought us peace was on him, and by his wounds we are healed. I take God's words and eat them like food. I believe it, I breath it, and bank on it. He has never failed me yet. He won't because His word is true.

Do we have that faith to know God is able?

Numbers 23:19: God is not human, that he should lie, not **a** human being changes his mind. Does he speak and then not act? Does he promise and not fulfill? Whatever He says He will do that, He will. God is qualified and more than able to do everything he says and more. God has supplied when we could not see a way out. He has opened doors where there were no doors. We had so many needs, but God has fulfilled every one of them and has never let us down. So, you see I can trust God in the good and bad times and in all my seasons. He is my shepherd I shall not have a need (Psalm 23).

Without faith, it's impossible to please God. -Hebrews 11:6

Lorraine Jones Whitfield

Pray or Worry, but You Can't Do Both

Trust in the Lord with all thine heart and lean not unto thine own understanding. (Proverbs 3:5)

When God promised Abraham and Sarah that they would be having a baby, they were both very old. They were put in an impossible situation. Abraham's faith didn't become weak, but he probably thought to himself, how am I going to do this, Sarah and I both are so old. Some things in our lives seem so impossible but with God all things are possible (Matthew 19:26). He just took God at his word and went on. Sarah, on the other hand, decided that she was too old, so she thought it was funny and laughed. But Abraham stood still and trusted God in it all.

> Whenever a situation seems almost impossible, the word of God says to lift our eyes to the hills from where our help comes from (Psalm 121:1).

Whatever your situation may be, and, in your eyes, it may seem so impossible, just know that God is able to do it. It may be your marriage, your children, finances, or maybe you think that the things of your past are so hard to get through. Just remember that God deals with the things that seem so impossible. Don't worry, because when you pray and then you worry it will not work and you find yourself still in that situation. Worry is like a rocking chair, it just goes back and forth and doesn't move. We don't need to know what God is doing or if he is going to do it, all we need to do is trust Him in all our situations. He will do whatever He says in His word. All things are possible to those that believe.

Notes

_____

_____

_____

_____

_____

_____

_____

_____

_____

_____

_____

_____

_____

_____

_____

_____

_____

_____

_____

_____

_____

_____

_____

_____

_____

_____

_____

In Everything Give Thanks

**Give thanks in all circumstances; for this is God's will for
you in Christ Jesus. (Thessalonians 5:18)**

There are so many things to be thankful for and we need to give thanks in all things. If we start making a list of the things in life we are thankful for, we may appreciate the big and small things in life. There are many things that we take for granted because we have such an abundance of them. There are people in countries like Uganda and many other countries are lacking and they would be wealthy if they had all the things we throw away; they would feel wealthy.

Some of these countries need food, clothing, and clean water. We have many means of transportation and ways to get around, but they walk, with no shoes, and must walk everywhere they go. When my children waste food or think they need the most expensive things to wear, I tell them to consider the children without. In all things they need to be thankful.

In the days of my youth, our parents would provide us with the food and clothing we needed. These things were not the fanciest ones or the most expensive types of clothing, but our needs were met. We had to eat all our food and couldn't waste any. If we didn't like something, we still had to eat it. We were thankful for our needs being met. My God shall supply all my needs (Philippians 4:19).

We should not just give God praise when things are going great. But give Him thanks always. Give thanks in everything: for this is the will of God in Christ Jesus concerning you (I Thessalonians 5:18).

Notes

_____

_____

_____

_____

_____

_____

_____

_____

_____

_____

_____

_____

_____

_____

_____

_____

_____

_____

_____

_____

_____

_____

_____

_____

_____

_____

_____

Spending More Time with God

Finally, my brethren, be strong in the Lord, and in the power of his might. (Ephesians 6:10)

John 15 says that abiding in Him is very important. We cannot do this without Him. We must be connected to his plan and purpose for our lives.

Spending time with God may seem hard for some and come easy for others. As we know when it's time to read His word, sometimes we get tired, sleepy, and distracted by everyday things in our lives. We never find the time until something happens. We need to put on the whole armor of God and be strong in the Lord and in His promises. Unless we abide in Him we are not connected. Being connected is being in His word and having that relationship with Him, following his commandments and meditating on His word. God has an individual plan for each of us and if we go to Him and abide in His word we will have that divine connection. Follow the word for yourself and try not to do what someone else does or try to become what someone else is. So finally, my brethren put on the whole armor of God (Ephesians 6).

My day includes prayer, intercessory prayer, worship, and praising Him.

There are days I fast as well as pray. Being like that tree planted by rivers of water that bring forth fruit in its season. Being able to read and study his word I consider to be a gift from Him.

By reading my bible, studying His word, and fellowshipping with the people of God in bible study, at church, and other things, we become strong in the Lord. Every day my time is different and by spending time with Him my relationship in Him is strong. Just allow God to direct your paths and lean not unto your own understanding.

Notes

_____
_____
_____
_____
_____
_____
_____
_____
_____
_____
_____
_____
_____
_____
_____
_____
_____
_____
_____
_____
_____
_____
_____
_____
_____
_____
_____
_____

Trusting God When You Don't Understand

**Though he slays me, yet will I hope in him; I will surely
defend my ways to his face. (Job 13:15)**

We must learn how to trust God when we don't understand, or when
we can't see any way out. We must trust God for our healing and deliverance. Psalm 46:10 says to rest in Him. In other words, to let it go and
allow God to move in our lives. Job had so many reasons not to trust
God, but he never lost his confidence nor his integrity. Job's children
were killed, and so was his livestock, but he never once complained
about the situation. Job faced a staggering series of crises and lost a lot
and did not understand what was happening and why God chose him
to go through these things. He decided that trusting God would be
easier than not.

There were times in my life that I may not have understood everything
God wanted to show me, but through many heartaches and trials I had
to learn to be still. I learned how to trust God when I had to trust God
after my car accident, when it felt like I lost everything. I felt destroyed
and cried more than enough. I had to dry up those tears and talk to
God. I had to empty out my heart and share my pain.

I almost lost my life, but God allowed me to see He was still in charge.
My healing was totally in His hands and in it all I had to trust Him.

In being still I had to realize that God is my refuge and strength, a very
present help in trouble (Psalm 46:1).

Notes

_____

_____

_____

_____

_____

_____

_____

_____

_____

_____

_____

_____

_____

_____

_____

_____

_____

_____

_____

_____

_____

_____

_____

_____

Faith Is Trusting God in Everything.

**For it is by grace you have been saved, through faith—
and this is not from yourselves, it is the gift of God—not
by works, so that no one can boast. (Ephesians 2:8-9)**

By faith we must trust God in all circumstances, which enables the believer to persevere and to remain steadfast in His word. We must trust God to help us through every situation daily. We must trust God when we are sick, for our healing (Isaiah 53:5) We must trust him for finances, and in trusting God. Faith is when we take God's word and pray it over our situation and believe for the outcome.

Faith without word is dead. When doing counseling and any type of ministry, I certainly need faith that will move mountains. When I travel from conference to conference or even to my workshops, I need mountain-moving faith for a great outcome. When setting up the conferences and workshops, I need faith when going out to speak to the ladies. I have faith that God will use my gift to help transform lives.

So, that "now faith" that is spoken about in Hebrews 11:1 is the substance of things hoped for and the evidence that we do not see. We know without a doubt that God will work something out in our lives.

Having that "now faith" means that we will trust God is in every situation and in all of our circumstances. This kind of faith leads to righteousness and seeks God and believes Him for everything. This faith is obedient to His commands and endures persecution. It has confidence in God's word and refuses to have any pleasure in sin. Faith is that steadfast trust in God and that His ways are correct. God says that His word will not come back empty and it will accomplish everything that He said it would. Trusting God in everything means that we will have no doubt that He can perform just what He says He can do. Habakkuk 2:4 says the just shall live by faith.

Notes

_____

_____

_____

_____

_____

_____

_____

_____

_____

_____

_____

_____

_____

_____

_____

_____

_____

_____

_____

_____

_____

_____

_____

_____

Don't Give Up

**Show me thy ways, O Lord, teach me
thy paths. (Psalm 25:4)**

Your situation may be a little tough right now and your circumstances may seem like they are uncontrollable but don't give up! Regain your territory and stop allowing the devil to steal from you. If necessary, take your city little by little. Joshua said to the people, "Shout, for the Lord says to take the city and do it on the seventh day" (Joshua 6:16). So, don't give up but allow God to direct your paths. When you pass through the waters I will be with you, they will not overtake you. When you walk through the fire it will not burn you (Isaiah 43:2). Whatever you may be facing or may be experiencing in your life—I am here to encourage you to get through it and never to give up! It is easy to let go and give up! It is easy to say "I QUIT"—it takes a little faith to get through it.

There were so many times I felt like throwing in the towel on everything. I felt like giving up at school, quitting my business, and just sitting and having that pity party. But there was this still small voice inside of me telling me to P.U.S.H. (Pray Until Something Happens). And that is what I did. I followed the direction of the Lord and continued to pray over my circumstances until a change came. I now have my Master's degree and other certifications because of it. I am working in my business and meeting new clients daily. I am so thankful for all that He is doing. God has been opening doors and making ways we cannot see. So don't give up.

Notes

_____

_____

_____

_____

_____

_____

_____

_____

_____

_____

_____

_____

_____

_____

_____

_____

_____

_____

_____

_____

_____

_____

_____

_____

_____

_____

And Ye Shall Know Their Fruit

But the fruit of the spirit is love, joy, peace, longsuffering, gentleness, goodness, faith, meekness, and temperance. Against such there is no law. (Galatians 5:22-23)

If you abide in the Lord and His word abides in you, we can bear much fruit. To everything there is a season and a purpose under the sun. We go through so many changes in our lives and in each season, there is a purpose and plan. John 15 talks about the branches and the vine and Jesus describes himself as that "true vine" and those who are his followers or disciples are the branches. If we are connected and remain attached to Him as our source of life, we will bring forth and produce much more fruit. We will be planted by the rivers of water that being forth much fruit in its season (Psalm 1:3).

In my life I often think about going through each season of life and learning how to stay connected to the true and living vine. When I think about bringing forth much fruit in my season—I think about having more love for my family and friends and the people around me—I think John 4:7-9. I think about and get excited when it comes to having more of Jesus and less of me and so I can bring forth much more joy and by abiding I will be able to be fruitful in God's presence.

I can remember first coming to Christ. I remember having an anger issue and I didn't know how to release myself from it. I dealt with it for many years, until one day I learned how to read, study, and pray more and more. I began to abide in Him and the word of God. I began to produce that fruit that Galatians 5:22 is talking about. I feel as if I am now like that tree by the rivers of water and these big roots that I have now I am stronger and my anger is controlled. Being able to abide in Him allows me to be fruitful and not fruitless.

Notes

_____

_____

_____

_____

_____

_____

_____

_____

_____

_____

_____

_____

_____

_____

_____

_____

_____

_____

_____

_____

_____

_____

_____

_____

_____

The Empty Nest

Weeping may endure for a night but joy cometh in the morning. (Psalm 30:5)

What is an empty nest? The term Empty Nest Syndrome refers to feelings of sadness or an emptiness one feels when children grow up and leave home. This condition affects both parents, but it is more often experienced by mothers. While many parents experience a sense of loss and distress, it can also be a time when you focus on taking control of your personal needs instead of those of your children.

Why am I saying this now? My house has been empty for years. The children had all grown up and now have their own children. I am leaving my house of 19 years and it is bittersweet. It is an emptiness, I feel as if I am leaving something behind. Maybe it's the memories. The many times I gave my children spankings in those bedrooms. The times my husband nursed me when I had surgery and taught me how to walk again in my living room. The crying from the pain in life and healing in my bedroom. I think about all the fun we had and games we played and birthday parties we had for all the children. The many nights I rocked them to sleep when they were sick. Yes, it's my own empty nest. Is it just leaving memories behind we made?

I was feeling like I was leaving those memories behind. I am taking them with me. The sadness of leaving that home will not compare to what lies ahead. God reminded me that the memories are pictures etched into your heart. Those are for me and to hold onto for the rest of my life.

Notes

A NEW THING

God says, Behold I will do a new thing now and it will spring forth, shall ye not know it? I will make a water in the wilderness and rivers in the desert. (Isaiah 43: 19)

My husband and I moved into an even smaller place in Wilson, NC. Transitioning was hard and letting go was, too. It is the perfect size for the both of us. Our empty nest years have given my husband and me time to reconnect and discover things we can pursue together. God took the emptiness I felt and gave me fullness.

It has opened new doors and has allowed us to be even closer in our marital relationship and with God. If you are struggling, try to look at your empty nest as an opportunity for something new in your life. Know that God has a plan and purpose for your lives. It may look empty, but it is really a full nest. It is filled with joy and lots of love. We are enjoying all the new things that God has promised us and it is springing up and we are excited about everything He has done. God is true to His word.

Notes

_____
_____
_____
_____
_____
_____
_____
_____
_____
_____
_____
_____
_____
_____
_____
_____
_____
_____
_____
_____
_____
_____
_____
_____
_____
_____

Are you faithing it?

For by grace are ye saved through faith; and that not of yourselves: it is the gift of God. (Ephesians 2:8)

Yea, a man may say, thou hast faith, and I have works: show me thy faith without thy works, and I will show thee my faith by my works. (James 2:18)

I know that faithing it isn't exactly a word in the dictionary but are you faithing it? The bible speaks of the "now faith." The kind of faith that can move mountains. The bible teaches us about the kind of faith that healed a lady that had an issue of blood for twelve long years and all it took was one touch from the master's hem of his garment. In Luke chapter 13 it tells about another lady that was bent over for 18 long years. They called it an infirmity. She struggled with this for a long time. I call her the woman that was bent out of shape. She was faithing it. She heard that there was a man that could heal anybody. He decided to see it his way. Jesus spoke to her situation, touched her heart, and ministered to that little girl inside of her. He said, "woman thou art loosed" and she was straightened up immediately. It was by her faith. So, you see, if she didn't believe and decided to doubt Jesus, she would still be bent out of shape. Then at the pool 38 years was a man that couldn't walk but was bedridden. By faith and trusting Jesus to just speak to his situation and "take up thy bed and walk," he did exactly that.

Faith without works is dead. We must trust God at his word. By faith I was healed from my issues and from many situations in my life. By faith God healed my mind after a miscarriage. I was faithing it and still do in my everyday life.

Prayer is the key and faith unlocks the door. This was a saying that the older ladies in the church used to say. When we pray we must believe, we must stand strong on His word and waver not. Prayer is a powerful tool and by praying and believing we are exercising our faith and by faith we know that God hears. This is how we invite God to get involved in out situations. We communicate to Him our needs and he supplies them by faith and through prayer. After we have prayed then we must walk by faith and begin speaking it into the atmosphere and doubt not. We must act as if we already got our answer.

I remember when I asked God to heal my body after having that issue and I knew that only He could heal me, by faith I prayed and trusted Him to remove that sickness and allow me to be free. I believed, and it came to pass. Trusting in and believing God for the things we cannot see but know that God is able to bring it to pass, by faith I was made whole.

Notes

_____
_____
_____
_____
_____
_____
_____
_____
_____
_____
_____
_____
_____
_____
_____
_____
_____
_____
_____
_____
_____
_____
_____
_____
_____
_____

If I Regard Iniquity in My Heart

**If I regard iniquity in my heart, the Lord will
not hear me. (Psalms 66:18)**

When my mom was about to transition to her new home, I remember praying the prayer of faith and believing God for healing her and I know that he did just what was asked of Him. I made sure my heart was cleared and I had forgiven because I wanted to be heard. It wasn't my will, but God's will be done and so was my mother's will. She was ready to move on. It was a sad day, but it was time for her eternal healing.

God says in Matthew 7:7 ask, seek, and knock. If we ask anything in prayer and believe, it shall be done. Prayer is the key component to talking to God. Prayer is our ultimate communication with Him. With prayer and faith, I found out that it can move mountains and heal cancer, and all manner of diseases. I know that prayer changes thing and the mind of God. Then we must look at it this way. If we have sin in our hearts, He will not hear our prayer. So, without a doubt I know God heard my prayer and healed her and took her home.

Notes

_____

_____

_____

_____

_____

_____

_____

_____

_____

_____

_____

_____

_____

_____

_____

_____

_____

_____

_____

_____

_____

_____

_____

_____

_____

Mountain-Moving Faith

**"Have faith in God," Jesus answered. "Truly I tell you, if anyone says to this mountain, 'Go, throw yourself into the sea,' and does not doubt in their heart but believes that what they say will happen, it will be done for them."
(Mark 11:22-24)**

I can remember asking God to move on my behalf. The doctor thought I had thyroid cancer and I told Him that I was healed and stood on God's word. I began to speak to that situation and trusted God for the outcome. After surgery was over and the results were released, the doctor said the tumor was benign. I praised God for the outcome because His word will not lie.

This passage of scripture also makes it plain to us. If we pray and don't forgive, he will not forgive us of our trespasses and therefore our prayers will be hindered. We cannot hold any animosity or bitterness in our hearts if we expect to hear from God. We must forgive and ask God to create in us a clean heart and renew the right spirit within us (Psalm 51:10).

Notes

All Things Work Together

**And we know that in all things God works for the good
of those who love him, who have been called according to
his purpose. (Romans 8:28)**

There are many things in our lives that makes us happy. To some money is one of those things. The small things in life that make me happy are my marriage, my children, my health, life, and especially the Lord. Some people find happiness in things. They find happiness in materialistic things. Those things that God says that will soon fade away. For some, happiness revolves around having many friends, relationships, and sports and games. As for me there are times I find peace and happiness in just a good old piece of chocolate candy. I seem to find enjoyment there. That is just one of my fleshly pleasures. There are times I go to the store and get that Milky Way and I find that peace eating that candy. But one thing for sure, it's not that perfect peace and it's just a temporary joy. I just enjoy eating it bite after bite and it's good until the end.

There are many things in life that can bring happiness but, in my life, I find a lot of my happiness in God. We all have personal issues that may turn our world upside down and we don't know which way to turn. We may cry, scream, shout, or depression may come upon some. Psalms 30:5 says that weeping may endure for a night, but joy comes in the morning. Our morning can be at any time. This scripture allows us to see that no matter what happens in our life, God will bring us through it. James 1:3 says to count it all joy. Then one may think how I can count this all joy when cancer hit our family. How can we count it all joy when death comes to our door? In other words, we must trust God because all things work together for the good of those who love the Lord (Romans 8:28). We must trust God no matter what it looks like. Weeping may endure for a night but know that God will dry up all our tears. He promised us that He will never leave us, nor will he forsake us. He will always be with us. So, you see God has promised us that there will be a time of joy in the midst of our storms. We must know that He is able to bring us through them.

The only truly happy people are those who have been forgiven for their sins. Happiness may come and go at times in our lives, but the joy of the Lord will bring true contentment. That piece of chocolate candy may bring me temporary happiness and give me pleasure for a short time, but real joy endures forever. It is everlasting. So, weeping may endure for a night, but joy comes in the morning.

Notes

_____

_____

_____

_____

_____

_____

_____

_____

_____

_____

_____

_____

_____

_____

_____

_____

_____

_____

_____

_____

_____

_____

_____

_____

_____

_____

_____

_____

Joy Comes in the Morning

Weeping may endure for a night,
but joy comes in the morning (Psalm 30:5)

In our lives we face disappointments, sadness, and issues. We can't escape them. That is a part of life. Some will go through mourning, but we can't avoid none of life's test, trials, or seasons. We must endure and embrace the storms in life. The Bible, Psalm 30:5, says that weeping may endure for a night, but joy comes in the morning. This is a part of life one must be able to endure. We must be able to deal with the heartaches, sadness, grief, and other emotions in our lives, but God promised us that if we could just hold on our morning is coming. We must learn how to let the spirit of joy back into our lives at the time of sadness and not allow guilt to come in and make us feel heavy about feeling enjoyment after our disappointments. The word of God says that He will keep us in perfect peace if we keep our mind on Him and if we trust him. He will give us the joy needed in the middle of our situation. But we must stay in touch with our emotions and realize that God is a healer and that trouble doesn't last always. We must trust that God can bring us through the situation.

There have been times that I have been sad because my mom is no longer here and I have cried without end. I have had dreams about her and the pain seemed to have no end. But God promised me peace in the midst of my situation and patience as I went through it. He promised me that everything would be alright. I can say that weeping has endured for a night, but joy came during my mo(u)rning. I can now rejoice and see that everything has a season and God has a purpose for everything under the sun. God knows what was best for my mother and I do not question that, but the pain it left us with and the hurt that we had to endure and the love that she showed us has no price. I was sad of course and my emotions may have been a little out of control, but I can now rejoice in the pain and suffering, and I know that my morning has come. My mourning has come, and I can see the joy in it all. I may have wept and sometimes still do, I may have my mourning, but again I know the true meaning of joy because God has taught it to me that this time I must go through and he has a plan and purpose for it all. I have joy in my mo(u)rning.

Notes

Be Thankful NOW!

And whatever you do, in word or in deed, do everything in the name of the Lord Jesus, giving thanks to God the father through Him. (Colossians 3:17)

Today we had a powerful prayer for those that were sick, shut in, and mentally disabled. We prayed for husbands and marriages. So, my question is, do you have a thankful attitude? Do you trust and believe that God can do all things but fail? Whatever we do in life we must give thanks for everything in the name of the Lord. Many people find it easy to be thankful when things are going well but quite another thing to give thanks when the world seems to be falling apart. We should praise God always and not just when there is a reason to do so. It is so easy to give thanks when we have a reason to, but we must be able to give thanks when it is a sacrifice to do so. If we took the time to make a list of all our blessings that God has given us, we would be quickly reminded of all the good things that he has done and all the many blessings that he has bestowed upon us. There are many things we take for granted because we have an abundance of them. I am reminded of the pictures my daughter shows us from her missionary trips and seeing how these children in Uganda live and how they praise God out of what they need. They have learned that God will supply their need. It looks like they praise and give thanks for things they do not see, and God always blesses them. I see their sacrifice of praise and the joys that they share because of the supplies and gifts that the missionaries bring to help furnish the schools. It is by faith and believing and trusting God, and in all things we must give thanks.

There are so many things we can be thankful for if we decide we are going to continue to offer up thanksgiving and try not to complain about our situations but to trust God in our healings and families. Praying and thanksgiving for everything he supplies in our lives.

Every day should be like Thanksgiving Day. We need to give thanks for all thing and be reminded that God is in total control of our lives. We should give thanks for the little things and the things we so forget, for example: breathing, eyeglasses, hearing aids, feet, and shoes to put on our feet. God is so good so in all things we must give thanks because this is the will of God.

Notes

The Fight of Faith

**The Lord shall fight for you, and ye shall
hold your peace. (Exodus 14:14)**

There will be things that we will have to encounter, and you will need the Lord to fight for you. We seek God to fight for us in our homes, our marriages, and with our children. The Lord told Moses to "fear ye not, stand still, and see the salvation of the Lord and those Egyptians whom we see then we will not see them again." God is telling us that whatever we may face in our daily walk, He will be with us if we walk in faith and trust Him in the midst of the battle. The Lord wants trust to hold our peace and trust him by faith that He will bring us through. God has assured his people that He will fight for us if we walk it out by faith (Hebrews 11:1). If we walk by faith God will fight for us. Without faith it's impossible to please God. The deliverance of Israel through the Red Sea confirmed God's promises that "He will fight for you" (Ephesians 6:10). We must put on the whole armor of God and be able to stand against the wiles of the devil. He wants us to be fully equipped in this battle. The Lord will take away from thee all sickness and put none of the evil diseases and He will deliver the enemy before thee: thou shalt smite them. God has us covered and he will bless us to get through any situation. The weapons of our warfare are not carnal but mighty through God to the pulling down of strong holds (2 Corinthians 10:4).

Notes

Power Scriptures

Whatever things you ask when you pray, believe that you receive them, and you will have them. And whenever you stand praying and you will have them. And whenever you stand praying, if you have anything, if you have against anyone, forgive him, that your Father in heaven may also forgive you your trespasses **(Mark 11:24–25)**.

Be kind to one another, tenderhearted, forgiving one another, even as God in Christ forgave you **(Ephesians 4:32)**.

Ask and it shall be given you; seek and you will find; knock, and it will be opened to you. For everyone who seeks finds, and to him who knocks it will be opened **(Matthew 7:7–8)**.

He who trust in his own heart is a fool, but whoever walk wisely will be delivered **(Proverbs 28:26)**.

Power Scriptures Continued

Behold, I will do a new thing; now it shall spring forth; shall ye not know it? I will even make a way in the wilderness, and rivers in the desert **(Isaiah 43:19).**

Let us not grow weary in well doing; for in due season we shall reap if we do not faint not **(Galatians 6:9).**

The Lord is my shepherd; I shall no want **(Psalm 23:1).**

The Lord is my light and my salvation; whom shall I fear? **(Psalm 27:1)**

Lord,

I just want to thank you for the opportunity to send your message in this book by faith we can speak to the mountain of our situation and God will move it (Mark 11:24-25). We must continue to walk by faith and not by sight. Lord help us to live a life with the sense of purpose and understanding of your calling you have given me. I lay down anything that is not like you such as pride, selfishness, and anything else that would keep us from moving forward in our lives. Lord please help me to walk and understand the calling that you have on my life. Take away any discouragement that we may have and replace it with love, joy, peace, and all the fruit of the spirit as it says in (Galatians 5:22).

Lord, I pray that nothing will draw me away from serving you or fulfilling the plan that you have for our lives. Give me a vision for my life and a strong sense of purpose. Thank you for the promises that you promised to deliver me from evil and work that is set up by the enemy and that I will put on the full armor of God (Ephesians 6:10-18). Thanks for putting the enemy under my feet (Ephesians 1:22). Lord let there be nothing covered in my life that will not be revealed (Matthew 10:26) and hidden that will not be known.

Lord, I know that you who have begun a good work in me, complete it (Philippians 1:6). Please give me patience to not give up but the faith that my mountains will be moved and cast into the sea. That I stand strong in the teaching and deliverance of your word.

Lord I want to thank you for my family and all their support and thank you for my friend Elease Dobbs, who encouraged me along this journey. This wasn't easy, but it was worth it. So, Lord thank you for everyone who encouraged me to move forward.

In all things I give you thanks.

In your Service,
Lorraine Jones Whitfield

Notes

_____

_____

_____

_____

_____

_____

_____

_____

_____

_____

_____

_____

_____

_____

_____

_____

_____

_____

_____

_____

_____

_____

_____

_____

_____

_____

_____

_____

About The Author

Lorraine Jones-Whitfield is the wife of Elder Carlton Whitfield Sr. Lorraine is dedicated to helping people live according to God's word and to walk in the purpose that God has called them to. She mentors, coaches, and consults in Marriage and Family and Children's Ministry. She is the CEO of Hannah's Heart Ministry.

Women have been blessed by Lorraine's online Women's Book, Family and Marriage Ministry and her ability to lead and guide women and youth through the written word, women's prayer breakfast, and Women's Empowerment and Transformational sessions and her AIT (Anointed Individual Training) Boot Camps.

Lorraine and her husband Carlton are parents of seven and grandparents of 14 grandchildren and have been married for over 35 years and reside in Wilson, North Carolina, where they work in the ministry and have a powerful marriage and family-counseling group together. Carlton is a pastor and is currently mentoring and instructing in God's word with an awesome online ministry and home-based bible-study group. They love to meet people where they are and reach them for God's glory.

www.lorrainejoneswhitfield.com

https://www.facebook.com/**lorraine. Whitfield**

email: hannahsheart7@gmail.com

Made in the USA
Columbia, SC
27 May 2024

35867239R00028